THE

10

PRAYERS

OF

NEHEMIAH

Examining Nehemiah's Winning Strategies

Paul A. Scavella

The 10 Prayers of Nehemiah

Copyright

Paul A. Scavella

All scripture quotations unless otherwise indicated are taken from the King James Version (KJV).

Cover design by Mr. Brian Rolle

Dedication

This book is dedicated to my parents Pastor Neville E. Scavella, and Mrs. Alwhyne L. Scavella.

FOREWORD

Prayer is not only requesting, communing and expressing life, "it is also readiness to receive life. Listening to God is as truly prayer as speaking to Him. "Be still and know that I am God," this also is prayer. In our time there is danger that the saints will be so busy serving that they have no time to listen."[1] Perhaps, one reason why we do not get more answers to our prayers is we do not wait in a quiet, receptive mood to learn the answer. Prayer is a divine dialog and encounter between God and man.

Ellen White postulates it nicely, "prayer is the unbroken union of the soul with God, so that life from God flows into our life; and from our life, purity and holiness flow back to God."[2] Prayer bridges the void that was created by sin, and it restores a union that was deceptively broken. Prayer gives meaning to, and define the relationship between God and humanity, hence God is Master and we are His stewards.

The book Prayers of Faith for Tough Times: Examining Nehemiah's Winning Strategies is one that demonstrates, the results of the prayer of faith, in a simple yet profound way. It highlights the priority and the power of prayer from one of the most proactive and passionate leaders of all times. Nehemiah not only prayed but followed God strategic leading, to make his requests a reality. He was practical in his approach to prayer. His prayer was the secret and the source of his success. In essence, prayer empowered an ordinary man to do the extra ordinary. Prayer was the weapon that he used, to be successful in his spiritual warfare against the devil and his agents.

Therefore, it is with joy and confidence, that I recommend this book to all church, members, leaders, officers and ministers of the gospel. It could be one of the best books you have ever read on prayer.

- Dudley Hosin,
Prayer Coordinator for Jamaican Union of Seventh-day Adventist

---

[1] Lyman Abbott; Moncure D. Conway and W. R. Huntington, *The Theology of Prayer The North American Review*, Vol. 186, No. 624 (University of Northern IowaStable, 1907), 337-348.

[2] Ellen White. *Steps to Christ* (Silver Springs, MD: Review, 1893) 98.

TABLE OF CONTENTS

ACKNOWLEDGMENTS

Prayer has been described as the breath of the soul. I thank God for parents who modeled prayer and made it an integral part of my life as a child. In addition to my parents, there are countless loved ones who have offered supplications to God on my behalf. How grateful I am for the specific ways in which they approached God for me!

The many hurdles crossed are testaments of the purposeful, sincere and powerful conversations with God. Prayer is a crucial element for the Christian. It is imperative to foster a relationship that will direct the child of God to an understanding of the true posture of prayer.

I thank Sir Cyril Fountain, and Dr. Richard Berry who took the time to read the manuscript and made invaluable suggestions that are incorporated in the final product.

Mr. Okell Damastus, technology specialist; Mr. Brian Rolle, graphic artist; and Pastor Sheldon Newton have skillfully guided the publishing process. I am indebted to their kindness.

My wife, Joan has been a faithful partner in the project.

INTRODUCTION

There is no time or place in which it is inappropriate to petition God. There is nothing that can prevent us from lifting our hearts in the spirit of earnest prayer. Whether you find yourself on a crowded street or in the midst of a business engagement, you can petition God. You can plead for divine guidance, as did Nehemiah when he made his request before King Artaxerxes.

A closet of communion may be found wherever we are. It is important that the door of one's heart stands ajar continually for the Spirit of God to enter. This signals the willingness to have Christ abide as the Heavenly Guest in the soul (https://m.egwwritings.org/en/book/820.9803, Ellen G. White).

 n 586 BC, King Nebuchadnezzar took the Israelites into captivity in Babylon. Their fate was inevitable as they had broken covenant with God and persisted in sin. However, sometime after, a remnant of the Jews returned to Jerusalem. What they found was heart-breaking. The once glorious city was in ruins. The majestic temple was destroyed, the walls are broken down and the gates were burned. There was utter destruction.

Without the fortified walls for protection, the remnant Jews were exposed to the attacks of enemies of all kind. Hence, they were not only broken physically, but they were also shattered emotionally and mentally. A city without walls and gates, one that lay in the rubble was a symbol of defeat, shame, and helplessness.

Our introduction to Nehemiah, a Jew, whose name means *"comforter of or appointed by Jehovah"* occurs at the Persian court where he faithfully served King Artaxerxes.

Though more than 1,000 miles away living a relatively comfortable and fruitful life, Nehemiah's heart was in Jerusalem. He remembered a great city on the plateau between the Judean mountains but those memories were far from reality.

Nehemiah was burdened for his beloved land and inquired about its state. The news was daunting and distressing. In fact, the story was so sorrowful, Nehemiah wept bitterly. He mourned for days. His heart was heavy. His knees were weak. His love and patriotism would not let him merely empathize. He could not look the other way hoping that someone else would fill the gap and do the hard work. Furthermore, God had already determined that through Nehemiah, He would do great and mighty work.

Faced with a crisis of great magnitude, how did Nehemiah move forward? How did he respond to a seemingly hopeless situation? Did he look within himself to find the innate power and inspiration he may have possessed? Did he turn to the books of knowledge written by the great scholars and thinkers of his time?

Nehemiah fasted and prayed. He did what some scorned and labelled as being simple-minded. Early on, he recognized three things:

1. He did not have the power within himself to prevail.
2. The ability to transform and rebuild Jerusalem was in prayer.
3. His connection to the infinite God was the only way he would succeed.

Are the odds stacked against you? Are you overwhelmed by life's Problems? Is your life in ruins? Do you face conflict day after day?

This study is designed to build your faith, help you find hope, courage, and strength to rebuild the areas in your life that have broken down. It will show you how to deal with pressure and conflict (within and without) and how to take decisive action when confronted with life's challenges.

May you be inspired to live and lead with honesty and integrity in your home, church, business, and all your endeavors.

The great God who heard and answered Nehemiah's prayers is eager to answer and guide you step by step in your seasons of crisis.

PRAYER # 1

Hear Me, O God

And said, I beseech thee, O LORD God of heaven, the great and terrible God that keepeth covenant and mercy for them that love him and observe his commandments:

Let thine ear now be attentive, and thine eyes open, that thou mayest hear the prayer of thy servant, which I pray before thee now, day and night, for the children of Israel thy servants, and confess the sins of the children of Israel, which we have sinned against thee: both I and my father's house have sinned.

We have dealt very corruptly against thee, and have not kept the commandments, nor the statutes, nor the judgments, which thou commandest thy servant Moses.

Remember, I beseech thee, the word that thou commandest thy servant Moses, saying, If ye transgress, I will scatter you abroad among the nations:

But if ye turn unto me, and keep my commandments, and do them; though there were of you cast out unto the uttermost part of the heaven, yet will I gather them from thence, and will bring them unto the place that I have chosen to set my name there.

Now these are thy servants and thy people, whom thou hast redeemed by thy great power, and by thy strong hand.

O LORD, I beseech thee, let now thine ear be attentive to the prayer of thy servant, and to the prayer of thy servants, who desire to fear thy name: and prosper, I pray thee, thy servant this day, and grant him mercy in the sight of this man. For I was the king's cupbearer (Nehemiah 1:5-11).

ehemiah could play no ordinary role in the mammoth task ahead. Comfortable in the king's palace, he could have ignored the plight of his fellow Jews. But as God had ordained, he would be the leader of God's mission of physical and spiritual restoration.

It is said that a wise man knows his limitations. Hence, Nehemiah's prayers to the One who holds infinite resources demonstrated his wisdom. He understood the enormity of the mission and his inability to do it alone.

Humility in Prayer and Praise

Nehemiah presented himself humbly before God. He lay flat on the ground with his face downward as a sign of submission and reverence. He gave God the glory He deserves. He expressed great awe as he remained in the presence of God's majesty.

Recognition of God's Unique Power to Help

In praising God, Nehemiah acknowledged Him as the God of heaven, sovereign and reigning supreme over all His creation including us mere mortals. He did not ponder from whence his help would come. Should he approach the false gods of Babylon? Should he try the new age thinking or philosophies of men? Nehemiah did not waver. Immediately, he consulted the God of his forefathers.

Covenant Keeping, Merciful God

Early on, Nehemiah speaks directly of God's mercy and the fact that God keeps covenant. He uses the very words Moses spoke in Deuteronomy 7:9 to the children of Israel: "Know therefore that the LORD your God is God; he is the faithful God, keeping his covenant of love to a thousand generations of those who love him and keep his commandments." Nehemiah was confident in God's faithfulness and the fact that He keeps His promises. He suggests that God will do exceedingly abundantly above what we can think or ask.

Such assurance should draw us near to God in anticipation of His extended hand of grace in our lives and every situation we face. Whether our rubble and ruins are physical, spiritual, mental or otherwise, God can intervene and rebuild the broken down walls.

Nehemiah's repetition of Moses' words is a signal that God seals his agreements with us and is ever willing to honour His obligations. He is faithful and infallible. With God, there are no abandoned promises. Nehemiah knew from Scripture that God had made a covenant with His people and so His faithfulness dictated He would keep the agreement. In other words, Nehemiah was saying that he and the people of Israel could trust God's binding promises of "I will."

> I will give to you and to your descendants after you, the land of your sojournings, all the land of Canaan, for an everlasting possession; and I will be their God (Genesis 17:8).

I will dwell among the sons of Israel and will be
their God (Exodus 29:45).

But I will remember for them the covenant with
their ancestors, whom I brought out of the land of
Egypt in the sight of the nations, that I might be
their God. I am the LORD (Leviticus 26:45).

God's promises of "I will" are never broken. He is a covenant
keeping God. His disposition does not change neither is His
power exhausted. Nehemiah had historical evidence of God's
faithfulness which he could reference. He knew God cannot lie
(Hebrews 6:18).

He pointed to those facts of history as he prayed to God being
well aware of the many covenants God made and kept – the
Noahic Covenant (Genesis 9:11), the Abrahamic Covenant
(Genesis 12:1-3), the Mosaic Covenant (Exodus 19:5-6), and the
Davidic Covenant (2 Samuel 7:12-17). He recalled God's
faithfulness to Abraham, the patriarch of many nations, His
Covenant with Noah that He would save him and his family and
to all humanity that He will never flood the entire earth again.
Three months after the Israelites left Egypt, God also made a
covenant with Moses to spare them if they were obedient to Him
(Exodus 19:5). The Ten Commandments are the foundation of
that covenant.

Moses spoke to the new generation of Israelites who were about
to enter the Promised Land. This generation did not experience
the Red Sea miracles and they did not hear firsthand the law given
at Sinai. Thus, Moses thought it necessary to let them know that
God keeps His covenants and He is merciful. It is remarkable that
God Almighty would consent to enter into covenant with us.

As we seek God to answer our prayers, an indispensable truth remains. It is one that has been avoided, denied, trivialized and even abandoned by many including those of faith. Yet, it stands firm. In Nehemiah's prayer, he highlights this truth, that God's mercy and covenant are not bestowed upon all mankind. Rather, they are reserved for those who love Him with all their hearts, minds, and soul, as well as His people who highly esteem and obey all of His commandments.

The Old Testament verse of Deuteronomy 7:9 parallels with Jesus' words in the New Testament:

> If you love me, you will keep my commandments (John 14:15).

> Whoever has my commandments and keeps them, he it is that loves me in (John 14:21).

> Jesus answered him, if anyone loves me, he will keep my word" (John 14:23).

> Whoever does not love me does not keep my word (John 14:24).

It is difficult to ignore the connection between loving Jesus and keeping His commandments. In fact, Jesus emphasizes the point four times. Furthermore, He does so at a significant time – a few hours before He was crucified. In a short time, Jesus would no longer be physically present with His disciples. Their resolve, and love for Him in an evil, ungodly world that sought to torment and kill them, would be tested by their keeping of God's commandments.

Essentially, the covenant God made here is a bilateral covenant between God and man. In other words, both parties are obligated to keep all the terms and conditions. Of note is the fact that the agreement is not only mutually binding but mutually beneficial. Hence, mankind's keeping of the commandments and loving God results in God's faithfulness. The two go hand in hand. Needless to say, the covenant ends if either party is unfaithful. Now, we have already established that God cannot lie and He always keeps His promises. There is no concern that God will renege on His word. The question is, will you?

If we desire to reap the benefits of prayer, we must love God and keep all His commandments.

Confession of Sin

After his initial praise and declaration of God's faithfulness, Nehemiah went a step further in demonstrating that the "great and terrible" God is approachable and compassionate. He asked God to pay attention to his prayer and to open His eyes to hear his prayer. Again, he humbles himself asking God to take notice of His people's plight. With a contrite spirit, he admits that his people had broken covenant. As if to say, "God, we don't deserve your mercy. We don't deserve your faithfulness. We have not kept our end of the bargain. We have sinned against you. We have turned to false gods and evil doctrines. We have failed to keep your commandments and have suffered the consequences."

Nehemiah left no stones unturned. He had no intention of hiding like Adam and Eve in the Garden of Eden who soon found out that nothing can be concealed from God. Everything lies open and naked before Him. Nehemiah was forthright. He admitted that they had dealt corruptly. They had not kept any of God's commandments, statutes or judgments. They were merely a rebellious people. Note, in his prayer, Nehemiah does not point fingers. He included himself and his father's house (his family, his clan). It's not that God did not know, but Nehemiah understood he had to come clean. He had to admit to God that they were wrong and He was right and just.

Repeat God's Word in Prayer

Nehemiah's tone changes in verse 8. His penitent confession of sin was over. Now, he was urging God to remember His promise that if the people turned away from their idolatry, sins, and evil ways, He will hear and heal their land. If ever there was a time Israel needed repairing it was then. They had to capture the attention of God if they were to ever be a secure people again. Only God could help to remove the emotions of shame and worthlessness. Nehemiah knew that, and so he threw himself at God's mercy seat and pleaded for grace and forgiveness.

Affirms the relationship

Unilateral covenants do not require relationships. However, bilateral agreements like the covenant God made with His people do. Nehemiah draws on that fact and reminds God that inspite of their disobedience and sins, they were still His people. In essence, he was affirming the relationship. He was saying, "God, these are the very people you loved so much that you redeemed them by your great power and your strong hand. After delivering them before, will you now leave them in danger and exposed them to their enemies and oppressors?" He asserts that God did great things for His people before and He has not changed. He is the same God and the Israelites needed His power one more time.

Presents His Need

Finally, Nehemiah asked God to help him to be successful as he led the mission. Interestingly, Nehemiah did not ask God if he was the one to lead. He saw the need. He understood the call and then asked God to bring him success.

From inception, Nehemiah knew what He wanted God to do. He was faced with a daunting task. His heart was heavy. He was worried. Nevertheless, the last thing Nehemiah did in this prayer was present his need.

We all need to draw near to God as Nehemiah did. Our approach must be one of humility in recognition that God is awesome and majestic. It is a privilege we have to come before His throne of mercy to find grace in the time of need.

As we face life's challenges and trying situations, we can learn a lot from Nehemiah's prayers and actions. Like the Israelites, many times we suffer the consequences of breaking covenant with God. Like them, we fail to keep His commandments, His judgments, and statutes. We do not honor our end of the bargain. Hence, God is not obligated to keep His. But can we still approach God for the mercy and grace we need when we have fallen by the wayside? When our sins, idolatry, and disobedience lead us into captivity, does God pay attention? Evidently, He does.

Nehemiah shows us how to approach God, life, and crises:

- Recognize who God is.
- Accept our helplessness and need for God.
- Humbly pray to God in submission calling on Him to listen.
- Confess our sins.
- Claim God's promises.
- Affirm our relationship with God.
- Present our needs.

QUESTIONS

1. God is approachable and a God of covenant. What is that covenant and what are the implications?
2. What are the conditions attached to God's covenant?
3. To what commandments does Deuteronomy 7:9 refer?
4. What can you learn from Nehemiah's approach to prayer, grief, and sin?
5. How is your approach to prayer similar to or different from Nehemiah's?

ACTIVITY

Set aside some time to focus on your needs and the needs of those around you. Are there critical areas that have broken down? Find a place of solace where you can cry out to God in humility and reverence for his help and mercy.

NOTES

PRAYER # 2

Ask and It Shall Be Given

And it came to pass in the month Nisan, in the twentieth year of Artaxerxes the king that wine *was* before him: and I took up the wine, and gave it unto the king. Now I had not been beforetime sad in his presence.

Wherefore the king said unto me, why *is* thy countenance sad, seeing thou ar*t* not sick? This is nothing else but sorrow of heart. Then I was very sore afraid,

And said unto the king, let the king live forever: why should not my countenance be sad, when the city, the place of my fathers' sepulchers, lieth waste, and the gates thereof are consumed with fire?

Then the king said unto me, for what dost thou make request? So I prayed to the God of heaven (Nehemiah 2:1-4 KJV).

ehemiah continued to serve King Artaxerxes from day to day, but he did so with a heavy heart. He was overtaken by grief. Interestingly, although Nehemiah had prayed to God, the situation did not suddenly turn around. His sorrow was not miraculously turned to joy. The problem in Jerusalem was not

resolved; the people were still exposed and desolate. Nothing had changed – at least, from the physical perspective. Nehemiah continued to be sad.

Of import is the fact that the Bible shares the specific date of the events to follow. This is significant because it indicates to us, that months after Nehemiah had prayed, there was no answer. He had a burden on his heart.

Have you ever had to wait a long time to get your prayers answered? You are in good company. Nehemiah and Daniel shared similar experiences. The Bible does not say why it took four months for Nehemiah to get an answer. But we know what delayed Daniel's answered prayers.

Daniel the prophet had a troubling vision concerning a great war (Daniel 10:1). Like Nehemiah, his response to trouble and conflict was too fast, mourn, and pray. He did so for three weeks. In the instant that Daniel prayed God sent an angel to explain the vision. However, the prince of Persia an evil spirit resisted him twenty-one days. Michael, the prince, had to intervene for Daniel to get the answer (Daniel 10:13). The point here is that delayed prayer is not unanswered prayer. Daniel discovered that, and so did Nehemiah.

Justifiably worried and downcast, Nehemiah went before the king. He was depressed. The burden was so overwhelming he could no longer hide it. He could not pretend anymore, and the king noticed. Of course, such an attitude in the courts of the king was an insult and a punishable offense. Nehemiah was petrified. He also knew that what happened next could determine his future and that of the Israelites.

What Nehemiah didn't know was that God in His infinite wisdom had orchestrated a masterful plan on behalf of His people. He used

Nehemiah's sorrow to reach the king, to break the ice and open the door for Nehemiah to get what was necessary to rebuild the walls of Jerusalem.

King Artaxerxes had no say in the matter. He could be considered one of God's divine helpers; (people God uses to help us reach our destinies). Such helpers often arrive, when we least expect, as answers to our prayers. They come at the right time and in the right place, but never by happenstance — only God-ordained.

It was God who placed the burden for Jerusalem on the heart of Nehemiah; that's why he found it difficult to brush it off, to leave it alone, to get it out of his mind. God intended to use Nehemiah and King Artaxerxes to accomplish His mission. All the while Nehemiah felt helpless, forsaken, and in the pits, but God was working behind the scenes putting it all together. For indeed, God's ways are not our ways and His thoughts are not ours.

One of the greatest favors we can do for ourselves is to take God out of our little boxes. Stop trying to get Him to operate the way we expect Him to. Ultimately, God will use whoever He so chooses to ensure that His will is accomplished. Therefore, God used King Artaxerxes. Consequently, at a time when Nehemiah's head could have been severed, the king's heart was filled with mercy and compassion. God placed Nehemiah in the hands of a king who was tolerant towards Jews.

In reply to the King's question about why he was sad, Nehemiah was honest and wise. He could have withheld his true feelings as many of us do and forfeit our chances to get help. However, because he was vulnerable and open about the dilemma of His people and his concerns, the king asked a direct question: "What do you request?"

What did Nehemiah do when the king asked that question? What would you have done? He prayed to the God of heaven. Instantly, he turns from talking to King Artaxerxes to consulting God the King of kings.

You may notice that throughout the book of Nehemiah, there is a pattern in the way Nehemiah handles stressful situations. He prays to the God of heaven, not Baal or any false gods, not his friends and family. He doesn't turn to any other source but the Most High God (Nehemiah 4:4; Nehemiah 4:9, 5:19, 6:9, 6:14, 13:14).

This time, it appears as if Nehemiah's prayer was done in the mind. He sought God's guidance without making any vocal utterances. He wanted God to instruct him how to proceed and how to answer the question posed by the king.

It reminds us somewhat of the prayers Jesus offered in John 11:41 and Luke 23:34, as well as Stephen's prayer in Acts 7:60. These were short, direct prayers made when they were under severe pressure, in fact, in life and death situations.

Evidently, we can pray anytime anywhere, aloud or in silence. Paul's exhortation in 1 Thessalonians 5:17 is to pray without ceasing. This does not mean we are to prostrate ourselves 24 hours per day. Instead, it suggests that in all our situations, we should include God. At times, we will fall on our knees, at other times we may assume another position that the moment requires.

God is interested in our circumstances at every moment of our lives. It will help if we remain conscious of the fact that God is not only universally present, but He is present in all of the matters that concern each individual. Wherever we are God is, not only our physical location, but He stands with us when we are mentally and emotionally depleted when our spiritual lives have hit rock bottom, when our financial position is negatively impacted or when our homes have fallen apart. God is ever present when our children have strayed, and life just seems not to work. He is there when you are under pressure, and your back is against the wall.

When you don't know what to say or do, follow Nehemiah's example. God is just as available when you prevail in prayer for hours as He is when you whisper a short prayer. The key is to do so sincerely, humbly and in recognition that it is only by God's might and power you will succeed. Nehemiah needed resources and wisdom. God has the infinite supply.

> If any of you lack wisdom, let him ask of God, that giveth to all *men* liberally, and upbraideth not; and it shall be given him (James 1:5).

> But my God shall supply all your need according to his riches in glory by Christ Jesus (Philippians 4:19).

God will send you a divine helper in your time of need. The wait may be protracted, but Nehemiah is a testimony that God answers prayer.

QUESTIONS

1. How was Nehemiah's response similar to that of Daniel's when faced with troubling situations?
2. What can you learn from Nehemiah's answer to the king's question in Nehemiah 2:4?
3. What three character traits of Nehemiah can you identify?
4. In light of what happened to Daniel and Nehemiah, how should you respond when your prayers seem unanswered?

<u>ACTIVITY</u>

Read Nehemiah 1:2-4 and Daniel 10:1-18. List the emotions each man experienced. How do they compare to your feelings when facing a crisis? Take the time to pray to God about your situation

NOTES

PRAYER # 3

Conflict Without

Hear, O our God; for we are despised: and turn their reproach upon their own head, and give them for a prey in the land of captivity:

And cover not their iniquity, and let not their sin be blotted out from before thee: for they have provoked thee to anger before the builders (Nehemiah 4:4-5).

ehemiah took on the leadership role of rebuilding the walls, he continued the habit of praying to God whenever he encountered challenges. And they were many. He exemplified the true spirit of a good leader.

It wasn't long before the enemies of the Jews got word that Nehemiah was starting a mammoth rebuilding project. Sanballat, Tobiah, and Geshem their fierce enemies felt it was their duty to provoke, oppose, hurl insults and make sniffing, malicious remarks to obstruct the work. They acted very much like those who overtly/covertly attempt to discourage us from moving forward.

These three were dream killers of the worst kind. Similarly, people may view one's plan as a destiny of failure. This was evident in the behaviour of Sanballat, Tobiah, and Geshem. Did they have a reason for reacting negatively to Nehemiah? Were they upset at Nehemiah for having the audacity to believe he could reconstruct the walls that were torn down and the gates that were burned? Yes, they were furious because Nehemiah had the foresight and temerity to even attempt such a great work.

Evidently, they found pleasure in the fact that Jerusalem was in ruins. They were happy the people were exposed to the elements, wild beasts, and the attacks of their enemies. How dare Nehemiah! Perhaps, a spirit of fear also instigated their attitude towards the Jews. What could they have been afraid of? That Nehemiah's mission would actually succeed? Jerusalem would rise from the ashes and become a great fortified city again. What could have stopped it anyway when God the ultimate leader was in charge?

Consider for a moment that sometimes our enemies' greatest fear is that we will accomplish our dreams and get ahead of them. Hence, they will do everything in their power, use every strategy they can find, and even cause us to yield our souls to him (the devil) in order to stop us. Resentment, jealousy, and covetousness are as cruel as the grave.

Nehemiah's Imprecatory Prayer

How did Nehemiah respond? Again, he resorted to prayer but of a different kind. Imprecatory prayers are those where God is asked to invoke evil upon or curse one's enemies. Throughout the Bible various people have offered these prayers. King David in particular did so:

> Let death seize upon them, and let them go down quick into hell: for wickedness is in their dwellings, and among them (Psalm 55:15).

Let them be blotted out of the book of the living, and not be written with the righteous (Psalm 69:28).

May their path be dark and slippery, with the angel of the LORD pursuing them" (Psalm 35:6) and "O God, break the teeth in their mouths; tear out the fangs of the young lions, O LORD! (Psalm 58:6).

Nehemiah was just as angry with his enemies as David was. His prayers were filled with cries for righteous judgment on those who defied God and His people. They were not personal utterances for revenge, but cries to the God of heaven for justice. They were pleas to the omnipotent God to intervene. Equally so, it was an acknowledgement that vengeance belongs to God. It was an acceptance that in themselves they could not change the hearts of men or stop the hands of the enemy. They needed God to make wrong things right. David and Nehemiah recognized God's sovereignty over all mankind – the weak and strong, wicked and righteous. Worthy of repetition is that Nehemiah and David were asking God for justice, not revenge.

Bear in mind that the rebuilding of the wall was not a project of the Jews and Nehemiah. It was God's work. Therefore, when Sanballat, Tobiah and their cohorts jeered and mocked they were in a true sense attempting to discredit God. When they criticized the wall and laughed saying that it would fall if a fox went on it, they were laughing at God and belittling His ability to do the great work. This incensed Nehemiah. How dare these men challenge the God of heaven? Furthermore, they provoked him to anger before the builders. In other words, they dishonored God publicly. If there was a chance that they could spite or shame God they would have. But they couldn't. In fact, in Jeremiah 7:19, God declares that this type of behavior is "to their own shame."

If the pressure of leading the rebuilding mission was not enough Nehemiah now had to deal with the scorn and taunting of his enemies. Yet, to his credit, Nehemiah said nothing to them. Do you notice the silence? He does not answer. Rather, he prays.

Some may say that imprecatory prayers contradict the teachings of Christ. In Matthew 5:44-48, Jesus exhorts His followers to love their enemies and pray for, not against them. Jesus Himself prayed for His enemies when He was crucified on the cross. He asked God to forgive them.

So are Christians supposed to pray imprecatory prayers? The views vary on this. However, the below excerpt gives further insight on the subject:

> In the **Imprecatory Psalms** the author calls for God to bring misfortune and disaster upon the enemies (Psalm. 5; 11; 17; 35; 55; 59; 69; 109; 137; 140). These psalms are an embarrassment to many Christians who see them in tension with Jesus' teaching on love of enemies (Matt. 5:43–48). It is important to recall the theological principles that underlie such psalms. These include: (1) the principle that vengeance belongs to God (Deut. 32:35; Ps. 94:1) that excludes personal retaliation and necessitates appeal to God to punish the wicked (cp. Rom. 12:19); **(2)** the principle that God's righteousness demands judgment on the wicked (Pss. 5:6; 11:5–6); **(3)** the principle that God's covenant love for the people of God necessitates intervention on their part (Pss. 5:7; 59:10, 16–17); and **(4)** the principle of prayer that believers trust God with all their thoughts and desires – (Chad Brand, Charles

Draper, Archie England, Steve Bond, E. Ray
Clendenen, Trent C. Butler and Bill Latta, *Holman
Illustrated Bible Dictionary* Nashville, TN:
Holman Bible Publishers, 2003.812).

Was Nehemiah right to ask God to never forget the sins of those
who opposed him? Was he on good ground to ask God for justice?
The fundamental principle Nehemiah, David and many others
who used imprecatory prayers established is that when we are
faced with opposition from our enemies, we should run to God in
prayer. He is the one who judges evil doers and vindicates His
people. Hence our prayers should not emanate from hearts that
are bitter and resentful requesting personal recrimination but that
God's justice will be executed.

QUESTIONS

1. Read Nehemiah 4:4-5. What do you believe motivated
   Nehemiah to pray like this?
2. How does the behavior of Nehemiah's enemies compare
   to that of Goliath in 1Samuel Chapter 17?
3. Does Matthew 5:44 condemned imprecatory prayers?
   Explain why or why not?
4. How do you respond when insulted, provoked, and
   discouraged? What have you learned from Nehemiah that
   can help you deal with these situations?

ACTIVITY

Honestly check your life to see if you have feelings of bitterness
and resentment for your enemies. When you pray, are you seeking
revenge? Read Hebrews 12:15. Pray and make a conscious
decision not to let bitterness grow in your heart.

NOTES

PRAYER # 4

Opposition Within

Also I shook my lap, and said, So God shake out every man from his house, and from his labor, that performeth not this promise, even thus be he shaken out, and emptied. And all the congregation said, Amen, and praised the LORD. And the people did according to this promise.

Moreover from the time that I was appointed to be their governor in the land of Judah, from the twentieth year even unto the two and thirtieth year of Artaxerxes the king, that is, twelve years, I and my brethren have not eaten the bread of the governor.

But the former governors that had been before me were chargeable unto the people, and had taken of them bread and wine, beside forty shekels of silver; yea, even their servant's bare rule over the people: but so did not I, because of the fear of God.

Yea, also I continued in the work of this wall, neither bought we any land: and all my servants were gathered thither unto the work.

Moreover there were at my table an hundred and fifty of the Jews and rulers, beside those that came unto us from among the heathen that are about us.

Now that which was prepared for me daily was one ox and six choice sheep; also fowls were prepared for me, and once in ten days store of all sorts of wine: yet for all this required not I the bread of the governor, because the bondage was heavy upon this people.

Think upon me, my God, for good, according to all that I have done for this people (Nehemiah 5:13-19).

When the enemy fails in his attacks from the outside, he then begins to attack from within; and one of his favorite weapons is selfishness. If he can get us thinking only about ourselves and what we want, then he will win the victory before we realize that he is even at work. Selfishness means putting myself at the center of everything and insisting on getting what I want when I want it. It means exploiting others so I can be happy and taking advantage of them just so I can have my own way. It is not only wanting my own way but expecting everybody else to want my way too (*Be Determined – Old Testament Commentary of Nehemiah,* Warren Wiersbe).

The rebuilding of the walls revealed several social ills and internal conflicts that threatened to halt the project. The Jews complained about the conditions they were living under – high debt, mortgages, and bondage – much like the economic realities we face in our times. These problems had a far-reaching impact and appear to have existed before Nehemiah became governor. The problems plaguing the society were many and it would take a man with the wisdom of God to bring reform and chart a way forward. Below are some of the major issues:

- Poor people who were disenfranchised and owned no land could not get food.
- Those who owned land and mortgaged it to buy food soon found that inflations was so high and what little they had was eroding.
- Some felt the taxes were too high but, they had to be paid. Hence they had to get loans to pay them. Unfortunately, they often lost the properties they used as security when they could not repay the loans.
- The all too familiar tune was played in this city; the wealthy Jews were exploiting the poor to get richer.

These deep grievances developed into a crisis during the time the wall was being built. It was a time of economic hardship. However, Nehemiah was up to task, not only physically but his character preceded him. He had dealt righteously in his position. He was honest and just. In fact, for the time He was working on the project, he, his relatives and his followers paid their own expenses and exacted nothing from the people. Unfortunately, while Nehemiah was living with integrity, some Jews were doing all they could to increase their fortunes. They were, selfish, greedy, and unjust.

Nehemiah was angry and no doubt frustrated. Once again the Enemy had tried to break the people's will. The unity of the people was severely challenged. He faced pressure from without and within. The problem could not be ignored. He had to turn his attention to this dire situation. He had to deal with the distress of the poor who were suffering at the hands of their own. The internal conflict had to end. Nehemiah knew if the problems persisted, no matter how high or thick he built the walls a city divided against itself would not stand (Matthew 12:25). The fear of God was necessary to touch the hearts of men and rid them of covetousness.

The guilty parties needed to be confronted. However, before Nehemiah rushed to pass judgment, he stepped back and consulted with himself (Nehemiah 5:7). His approach was exemplary. Whether we have clear evidence of wrongdoing or not, we should think before we are swift to contend. Self-control is clearly the primary attribute on display here.

Finally, Nehemiah confronted the oppressors privately. When that didn't work, he called a public assembly to address the matter; it required a national conversation. There, He rebuked the leaders (Nehemiah 5:8). The people agreed to stop their usury and oppressive policies. That was progress Nehemiah should have been proud of. To have persuaded the people to stop is never easy. Nehemiah wanted a more binding agreement. He shook His lap and prayed. What was the significance of shaking his lap?

> The Hebrew word translated "lap" designates the lap of the garment, in which things were sometimes carried. The word is found only here, and as "arms" in Isa. 49:22. To emphasize the binding nature of the promise, Nehemiah performed a symbolical act. This consisted in his gathering up his garment as if for the purpose of carrying something in it, and then shaking it out— as he uttered the curse of v. 13. Among the nations of antiquity few things were so much dreaded as falling under a curse. The maledictions of Deut. 28:16–44 were similarly designed to impress those

who might be tempted to violate the law. Curses inscribed over the entrances to the tombs of Assyrian and Persian kings were intended to frighten away would-be looters. Ancient treaties were similarly protected against violation. Nehemiah's curse is unusual, but its purpose is clear (*http://mediaset.sdasofia.org*).

Once again, Nehemiah approached the God of heaven to take charge of the situation. God was the final judge. The one who would enact punishment if the promises were broken and the agreement violated. Again, we see Nehemiah's complete dependence on God to take control of every situation.

It's one thing to make a vow to man , but a completely different story when making a vow to God. In fact, the wise King Solomon warns:

> When you make a vow to God, do not delay to fulfill it. He has no pleasure in fools; fulfill your vow. [5] It is better not to make a vow than to make one and not fulfill it. [6] Do not let your mouth lead you into sin. And do not protest to the temple messenger, "My vow was a mistake." Why should God be angry at what you say and destroy the work of your hands? (Ecclesiastes 5:4-6 NIV).

In verse 19, Nehemiah asked God to remember him according to his good deeds he had done to the people. Nehemiah's style of leadership was unusual at that time. He was a servant-leader, rather than a dictator. He refused to place unfair burdens on the people or take their money to increase his riches. In those times, the people usually had to pay money to those who led whether they had or not – by any means possible. But Nehemiah did not rule like that. Instead of looking to the people for his rewards, he looked to God. For it is God who promised to reward us for our good deeds. Therefore, Nehemiah was calling on the great rewarder to do to him as he had done to the people. Amazing! This speaks volumes about Nehemiah's character and integrity. That he could go before the all-knowing, all-present, almighty God and make such a request is remarkable. Only those with clean hands and hearts can do that. Only those who act justly, love kindness and walk humbly before God, can dare do that.

Can you say God, remember me according to how I have dealt with the members of my congregation? Lord, remember me according to how I have dealt with my family, husband, wife, children, parents? Can you say God, remember me according to how I have dealt with the elderly, the poor, weak, and lonely?

Nehemiah led his people by the principle of seedtime and harvest. He recognized that whatsoever we sow, we will reap. And harvest time always comes. This was his harvest time and he was confident God would never forget his labor of love.

QUESTIONS

1. How would you describe Nehemiah's leadership style?
2. After reading about Nehemiah, if faced with a similar situation how would you deal with it?
3. How do you feel Nehemiah's character helped him to resolve these conflicts amicably?
4. What did you learn about the destructive power of internal conflict?
5. What great work are you doing for which you feel unappreciated?

6. What should be your attitude when your hard work is overlooked?

ACTIVITY

Write down five things you did when you last encountered conflict in your home, business, church etc. and how you dealt with it. Search the Bible for scriptures related to conflict that will help you better handle it the next time around.

NOTES

PRAYER # 5

Strength in Weakness

For they all made us afraid, saying, their hands shall be weakened from the work, that it be not done. Now therefore, O God, strengthen my hands (Nehemiah 6:9, KJV).

rogress was made. Nehemiah had already rebuilt the walls but the gates and the doors were not yet constructed. Fearful of the success of the Jews, Sanballat, Tobiah, and Geschem continued their schemes to discourage the people and stop the work. Their strategy was the very one Satan used in the garden of Eden and the one he continues to use on us today – to play with their minds. This deceitful trio continued to speak negative words to break the spirit of the workers. They knew full well that if you can break a man's spirit and kill his motivation, you have essentially won the war.

The spirit of a man will sustain infirmity, but a wounded spirit, who can bear? (Proverb 18:14).

As Christians, we should be protective and selective when it comes to our minds. Those of us who have been wounded and broken by the words and actions of others can attest to their potency. Words are never just words. They produce life or inflict death (Proverbs 18:21). Israel's enemies were attempting to kill their dreams and visions to stop the great work. In your life – if you haven't already – you will encounter those who use their mouths and the power of their tongue to inflict pain and to destroy your vision for your family, career and ministry. They will use their words to kill your spirit and weaken your hands. God's wisdom and the ability to discern are critical, particularly in times like these.

Nehemiah needed a discerning spirit in the midst of deception, lies, and conspiracy. Otherwise, he would have fallen into the snares of the enemy and led his followers into the same pit. Nehemiah could have bitten the bait when his enemies presented him with seemingly innocent proposals. Cunning and conniving were they with their letters, invitations, and suggestions; their sole intention was to steal, kill, and destroy.

Nehemiah's constant communication with God enabled him to discern that several letters from Sanballat were actually meant to threaten them and confuse their minds. They were playing mind games in an effort to frighten and conquer. They figured if they could instill fear in the heart of the leader and the people, the great work would stop. Strike the shepherd and the sheep will scatter (Zechariah 13:7).

If there is one emotion that can stop a great work it is fear. It is often triggered by a perceived threat. In this instance, Sanballat warned the Jews that their rebuilding of the wall was a sign they were plotting to revolt. He suggested that once the king heard, they would be in big trouble. That was enough to frighten Nehemiah if he didn't know better, if he weren't an astute, righteous leader who prayed to the God of heaven.

Fear causes us to act impulsively; it affects our ability to think and make sound decisions. That was the exact effect Sanballat was hoping for. The letters were written to have the Goliath-effect, to weaken their minds; thus, weaken their hands and make them run scared. In other words, paralyze them with fear that they could do nothing. Hence, the great work would cease.

So relentless was the enemy that he tried scheme after scheme and plot after plot to stop the great work. His intrigue and intimidation did not work so he resorted to slander and character assassination. They spread malicious rumors that Nehemiah had hired prophets to proclaim he was the king. This was a new tactic to get Nehemiah to negotiate; if he did not want the king to hear he should meet with them.

With heavenly wisdom Nehemiah declined the invitation to meet and discuss knowing that an enemy is an enemy. No matter how he attempts to transform himself into an angel of light, his sole objective is evil. God gave Nehemiah the prudent answers to their letters.

In the midst of trouble, Nehemiah once again turned to God. This time, he asked God to strengthen their hands. Nehemiah was direct and assertive. The enemy wanted to weaken their hands, so he asked God to do the opposite – strengthen their hands. What blessed assurance to know that we can approach the great God of heaven for relief, strength, wisdom, and comfort.

In our Christian walk, as we are faced with conflicts without and within, this simple prayer is enough to soothe us and quell our fears. In times of temptation, we can ask God to strengthen our hands. Asking God to be our strength is an acknowledgement of our weaknesses and an acceptance that He holds all power. In fact, apostle Paul, a faithful follower of Christ was aware of his weaknesses. He had a "thorn in the flesh," which he asked God to remove. God replied: "My grace is sufficient for you, for My strength is made perfect in weakness" (2 Corinthians 12:7-10).

As Nehemiah and Paul recognized, our true source of strength comes from God. Significantly, in this instance, Nehemiah did not ask God to remove Sanballat and his other enemies. He did not ask God to weaken their hands or stop them from hating His people and despising their efforts. Rather, He asked God to do a work in him. (Lord Transform Me)You will note that God did not remove the thorn in Paul's flesh. He also did not let Nehemiah escape the conflict and humiliation. Instead, He strengthened their faith.

QUESTION

1. Would you have handled this situation differently? Why or why not?
2. When faced with uncertain situations how do you decide what to do?
3. What can you learn from Nehemiah in this situation?
4. How does Mathew 10:16 help you to deal with situations like the one Nehemiah faced?
5. What leadership skills did Nehemiah display in his handling of this matter?
6. What spiritual gifts did Nehemiah display in this situation?

ACTIVITY

- Identify the problems, threats and fears in your life that have weakened your hands, killed your spirit and killed your vision.
- Pray to God for renewed strength and wisdom.
- Meditate on (2 Timothy1:7).

NOTES

PRAYER # 6

Think Upon My Enemies

My God, think thou upon Tobiah and Sanballat according to these their works, and on the prophetess Noadiah, and the rest of the prophets, that would have put me in fear (Nehemiah 6:14).

Christians should always expect fierce opposition. We would be fool-hearted to do otherwise. The Devil will not relent. He will do everything and anything to force us to compromise, hide, be silent and intimidated. Whether the opposition is political, religious, cultural, communists, militant atheists, secular humanists, terrorists, opportunists, sexists or others, it is inevitable. Jesus Himself told the disciples not to be surprised if the world hates them because they first hated Him. In our contemporary times, we should remember those words. However, we should also closely examine the words of Nehemiah and two profound questions he asked in Nehemiah 6:11 after another plotted against him.

1. Should a man like me run away?
2. Should someone like me go into the temple to save his life?

Nehemiah was not here referring to his physique, his intelligence, or his social status when he says "a man like me." He was addressing a more pertinent issue – his character. He was saying "why should I run away and hide? Why should I be ashamed and fear for my life? My character speaks for itself. I have served my God and my people with honesty and integrity. I have been just and transparent in my actions. All these accusations against me are false." Can you say that? Or would you have to flee?

After fierce opposition, Nehemiah was no doubt tired and frustrated. Yet, he persevered. All attempts to distract and weaken him had failed. Not because of his obviously strong leadership skills but because he prayed to the God of heaven.

In his prayer, once again, he uses the principle of seedtime and harvest (Nehemiah 6:14). Earlier, we highlighted his prayer asking God to deal with him according to how he dealt with His people. Here, Nehemiah gives a similar prayer. This time, he asks God to deal with his enemies Sanballat, Tobiah, Noadiah (false prophetess) and the other prophets according to their works. That is according to how they dealt with His people. Again, he surrenders to the God of heaven who knows the heart of every man.

Nehemiah's prayer suggests that he was also up against those who had no divine calling but pretended to be prophets in the land. They were the enemies within – walking, eating, and fellowshipping with the people pretending to be who they were not. Each day, they busied themselves spreading lies, stirring up strife, discrediting the leaders and trying to turn the people away from the voice of the true prophet. Does this sound familiar?

This is a telling reminder to put on the whole armor of God to stand against the wiles of the Devil, for even within the church there are false prophets, ferocious wolves in sheep's clothing busying themselves to divide and conquer. Jesus warned us about that very thing. He also teaches us how to identify false prophets – by their fruit you shall know them (Matthew 7:16-20).

Nehemiah strengthens his case against his foes by saying "that would have put me in fear." Fear was, indeed, the weapon his enemies tried to use to stop the great work. Nehemiah was saying to God, "They would have stopped the project if..." Nehemiah admits that the potential was there, the possibility existed that he could have succumbed to fear. He did not present himself as super human but human – open to failure. If he did not pray to the God of heaven, if he did not have the God-given spirit of discernment, if he did not know better, they would have succeeded in their evil plot. No wonder Jesus teaches us to be harmless as doves, yet, wise as serpents! (Matthew 10:16).

The difference between Nehemiah's prayer for himself and his prayer for his enemies is the outcome, the end result. Simply, you can only reap what you sow. Nehemiah's enemies sowed seeds of discord, conspiracy, lies, resentment, and malice. They tried to obstruct the work of God. Consequently, they would reap what they sowed. In God's time, they would receive exactly what they deserved – just recompense for their actions.

Nehemiah never threatened his enemies, he did not retaliate or plot against them. He never made a single attempt to vindicate his character. He simply surrendered them into the hands of God. In doing so, he freed himself from the mental turmoil, the emotional burdens, and spiritual decadence that come from seeking revenge. A peace emanated from Nehemiah because he knew that God was in control.

QUESTIONS

1. Why did Nehemiah ask God to think upon his enemies?
2. What did he mean when he asked God to "think upon my enemies."
3. Why was Nehemiah able to stand his ground when told about threats on his life?
4. Define integrity and its importance in leadership?
5. What would have happened to Nehemiah if he had fled to the temple?

6. How would your family, friends, work mates and those close to you describe your character?

ACTIVITY

Read Micah 6:8, Galatians 5:22-23 and 1 Corinthians 13:4-7. List all the characteristics you find pertaining to good character and prayerfully strive to have them.

NOTES

PRAYER # 7

―――

Revival

Then stood up upon the stairs, of the Levites, Jeshua, and Bani, Kadmiel, Shebaniah, Bunni, Sherebiah, Bani, *and* Chenani, and cried with a loud voice unto the LORD their God (Nehemiah 9:4, KJV).

ehemiah Chapter 8 gives an account of the events that led up to this point. After the reading of the law, the people were excited but also sorrowful. The law exposed their wrongdoings and only a few years after signing a covenant with God, they broke it. However, it is to their credit that after the book of the law showed them who they really were, they acknowledged their sins and repented.

James 1:23-24 compares the Word of God to a mirror, which lets us see what we look like. The mirror reveals our external features, while the Word of God reveals who we are on the inside. However, the challenge for many of us is what we do once we are exposed. What do we do when we recognize we have sinned against God, broken His covenants and failed to keep His commandments? Do we repent like the Israelites or are we like the man who looks in the mirror, temporarily sees himself, walks away and does nothing to make the necessary corrections?

You will notice that Nehemiah examined himself before he confessed the sins of the people. Resulting from this leadership trait, the people are now confessing their own sins and those of their fathers.

It is interesting that they were repenting at a time when they had been victorious, had resolved their conflicts and had seemingly grown as a people. However, the law forced them to reexamine themselves in light of God's requirements. Having done so, they recognized they had fallen short and all their righteousness was like "filthy rags."

In spite of all they were doing – busying themselves with building the walls, practicing certain rituals and participating in certain religious activities, they had fallen short. It took the reading of the law to show them their wretchedness.

Needless to say, we should be very careful not to confuse being busy doing the work of the Lord with being in right standing with God. Many continue to work in the ministry although the Spirit of God has long left them. We can be involved in ministry, plan the biggest conferences and seminars, have large followings in our churches and on social media sites, as well as attend church regularly; yet, we may have broken covenant with God and failed to keep all His commandments.

The appeal is for us to read the Word of God daily. Let it be a lamp unto our feet and a light unto our paths. The advantage we have in our modern societies is that we have easy access to the Word. We need not wait for scholars like Ezra to open the book and acquaint us with what God desires of us. We can do it ourselves.

Not only did the Israelites assemble to hear the words of the Law, confess their sins and repent, they also worshipped.

"They cried out with a loud voice to the Lord" tells us a lot about how the people were led in praise and worship. This was no quiet assembly in whispered tones. Those who led raised their voices in a prayer that included praise, adoration, confession and repentance. What is interesting is that the prayer is only about six minutes long. What is the lesson that can be derived from this? Effective prayer is not necessarily lengthy.

It is noteworthy that Nehemiah's prayer is similar. They begin by praising God. He is called the God of all creation. As the leaders worshipped the people were encouraged to stand and get involved. The leaders didn't do it alone. "Stand up and bless the Lord." It was not a time for those on the pulpit to shout praises while the congregation fiddled their thumbs and became distracted by the events around them. By the same token, the leaders led the worship. The people saw and heard them engaged in worshipping God. They did not sit comfortably as the congregation worshipped. They did not read the book of the law with their heads down as the congregation worshipped; they actively participated in the very thing they wanted the people to do. Collectively, they praised God.

Also, as they stood on the pulpit they encouraged the congregation to stand as an expression of worship. It was showing reverence in the presence of God as seen in Exodus 33, when the people stood every time the presence of God was at the entrance of the tent meeting. Similarly, in 2 Chronicles 20:5, Jehoshaphat stood in God's presence and called upon the Lord.

The people were obviously obedient to the call to stand and worship. They exalted God's name above all others. They affirmed His Lordship. They acknowledged He created the heavens, the earth, the seas and everything in them and he sustained them by His awesome power.

Like Nehemiah's prayer, they pointed to history and spoke about God's covenant with Abraham and his descendants. They praised God for keeping His promises, delivering them from slavery performing miracles and keeping his promises. They praised God for seeing their affliction and showing compassion. They were testifying of the greatness of God to their forefathers. They were telling of His trustworthiness and His track record of keeping promises. God led, fed, and protected them.

Significantly, they mention God descending on Mount Sinai to speak with them from heaven, to give them "just ordinance, true laws, good statutes, and commandments." Furthermore, they emphasized the fact that God made His holy Sabbath known to them and commanded them to keep His precepts, statutes and laws. They honored God for loving them enough to reveal His expectations of them. How could mere mortals understand what God expects unless He loves them enough to reveal it? How could God judge His people if they have no guidelines to live according to His desires?

The Ten Commandments were given by God to reveal His will to mankind. They are the expression of His desires. He wanted human beings to know how we should relate to Him and others. Hence, the Israelites had no excuse when God chose to pass judgment – neither will we.

Like Nehemiah's prayer, the leaders confessed the ingratitude displayed by them and their forefathers after all God had done for them. They confessed the indifferent attitude they displayed. They admitted the people were proud and refused to keep God's commandments. It is interesting that their refusal to obey God's commandments is reflected in their acts of rebellion.

The leaders continued their prayers by contrasting their evil ways with the mercies of God. Nehemiah 9:17 begins: "**But** You *are* God, ready to pardon, gracious and merciful, slow to anger, abundant in kindness, and did not forsake them.

The conjunction "but" can create excitement or remorse depending on what follows. It generally contrasts what was written or said before to what came after as seen in the following verses:

> Yet your father has deceived me and changed my wages ten times, **but God** did not allow him to hurt me (Exodus 31:7).

> For indeed he was sick almost unto death; **but God** had mercy on him, and not only on him **but** on me also, lest I should have sorrow upon sorrow (Philippians 2:27).

After their overt rejection of God's word, their rebellion and idolatry, they could still testify of God's mercy and grace, as well as His willingness to pardon. What a wonderful testimony of a loving God who in spite of our failings will constantly reach out to us. Even though we have turned our backs on Him and gone our own way He is willing to hear our cries.

The Israelites were like many of us who have rejected God's Word for the pleasures of sin. Yet, God is merciful and ever ready to pardon when like the Prodigal we come to our senses.

When you come to a point in your life that you realize you have messed up, you have broken God's laws and commandments, you have broken the bilateral covenant with God and you have not loved Him with all your heart, mind and soul, it can spark a revival within. It can be a new beginning for you and your relationship with God.

The Israelites were at that point and after praising, reflecting on God's goodness, confessing, and repenting, they had to make a decision. After looking in the mirror (the Word) and seeing their sinfulness, would they walk away and continue to defile their garments or would they yield to the living God? They chose the latter.

> And because of all this, we make a sure *covenant,* and write *it;* our leaders, our Levites, *and* our priests seal *it* (Nehemiah 9:38).

Israel made a covenant with God. They committed themselves to obey His commandments and follow His ways. Our moments of decision to accept or reject God will come. Which way will you choose? Reading the Word, honest self-examination, and reflection on God's goodness lead to repentance.

QUESTIONS

1. What covenant did the people break according to the book of the Law?
2. How did they realize they had fallen short of God's will?
3. How did the people respond after their revelation?
4. Name three things the people showed God gratitude for?
5. Why do you think they mentioned God giving the Ten Commandments on Mount Sinai in their prayer?
6. What is the purpose of the Ten Commandments?
7. What should be our response when the Word of God reveals sin in our lives?

<u>ACTIVITY</u>

The reading of the Law sparked revival and renewal in the lives of the Israelites. Spend more time reading God's Word and asking God for renewal and revival in your life.

NOTES

PRAYER # 8

———

Remember Me

Remember me, O my God, concerning this, and wipe not out my good deeds that I have done for the house of my God, and for the offices thereof (Nehemiah 13:14 KJV).

 arlier, we see Nehemiah asking God to remember him according to what He had done to His people. Again, Nehemiah makes a bold request. This time asking God to remember "this" (in reference to Eliashib and Tobiah) and all that he had done for the house of God and His service.

Written in the book of Moses that was read aloud in the assembly was a law that forbade any Ammonite or Moabite from entering the assembly of God. The law was established because these said people refused to meet the children of Israel with bread and water in the wilderness. Instead, they hired Balaam to curse the Israelites. God had promised Abraham that those who cursed Israel will be cursed by Him but those who blessed Israel will be blessed by Him. Therefore, the Moabites and Ammonites were under God's curse.

And I will bless them that bless you, and curse him that curses you: and in you shall all families of the earth be blessed (Genesis 12:3).

Eliashib the high priest was in charge of the storerooms in the house of God. You would think that if there was somebody you could trust, it would be the high priest, Israel's supreme religious leader. Moreover, the high priest was not only expected to be whole without physical abnormalities but He was to be holy in his conduct. He was to be an example to the priests under him and the people. However, Eliashib, who must have known better, acted deceitfully and aligned himself with Tobiah, the Ammonite who conspired with Sanballat to stop the wall from being built.

What Eliashib the high priest did was the highest level of abuse of authority and betrayal one could encounter. He allowed Tobiah to take over the storerooms in the temple for his own use. These were no ordinary rooms. They were set aside exclusively for the grain offerings, offerings for the priests, as well as the new wine. However, the enemy was given full access to the temple and sacred vessels of God by the high priest – of all people.

The law said an Ammonite was not to enter the congregation. How then could the high priest of Israel allow one of the greatest enemies of Israel into the temple? Furthermore, how could he remove the sacred things of God from the temple so that Tobiah could be comfortable? Eliashib seemed to have lost fear for God and respect for the house of God.

While Nehemiah was absent from Jerusalem for over ten years, the enemy took the opportunity to defile God's house and desecrate His holy things. He used the person to whom God entrusted His house to turn it into the comfort zone of the enemy.

On his return to Jerusalem, Nehemiah discovered Eliashib's evil. After the initial shock and grief he experienced, Nehemiah took aggressive, affirmative action.

1. He threw out all of Tobiah's household goods.
2. He commanded that the rooms be cleansed.
3. He brought back the articles of the house of God, with the grain offering and the frankincense.

Nehemiah's swift and decisive action should not be overlooked or taken for granted. It is the type of action we need to take when sin enters our lives. We must see the dangers we are exposed to. Immediately and decisively throw out whatever defiles us from our hearts, ask God to cleanse us and return God to his rightful place in our hearts. Ignoring evil in the temple of God has dire consequences.

Jesus Himself took similar action in the New Testament when He threw the money changers out of the temple (Matthew 21:12). They, like Eliashib had profaned the temple of God. Evidently, it takes bold action to get rid of the evil, not passive requests for compliance.

But there were other serious matters Nehemiah had to put right. The Levites and the musicians, God's special ministers were to be paid a tithe so they could support themselves while in God's service. However, because the people disobeyed the law, and failed to give, the Levites had to return to the fields to support themselves. Consequently, the house of God was neglected.

Knowing this situation had to be corrected, Nehemiah gathered the rulers together and "set them in their place." He rebuked them and set things in order. Subsequently, the people reverted to faithful financial stewardship. Nehemiah set up a system that was sustainable. He selected competent, trustworthy individuals to oversee the distribution of the tithes that would support the Levites and musicians thus functioning as prescribed by God.

Nehemiah had an impressive summary of what he had done, and he asked God to remember the people. And why not? The God of heaven whom he served promised to reward those who diligently seek Him. In presenting his case, he was asking God not to forget His faithfulness and loyalty to His house and its service.

Nehemiah was exceptional in his commitment to God and his dedication to His work. While others did nothing when the house of God was being defiled and the enemy was establishing his kingdom Nehemiah took a stand. When the Levites and musicians were being robbed of what was rightfully theirs, Nehemiah stepped in and rectified the situation.

The situation that existed was not a secret. The rulers and the people knew that the house of God was being defiled. They also were aware of the dire circumstances under which the Levites and musicians lived. Yet, they chose not to support the men and women of God and to neglect His house. No one but Nehemiah seemed willing, interested or able to fix the situation.

Asking God to remember him was neither being pious nor boastful. In humility, he simply asked God to remember him, his passion for His house and his good deeds. In any case, God promises not to forget our labor of love.

QUESTIONS
1. How was this prayer different to the one in Nehemiah 5:19?
2. Why were the Moabites and Ammonites forbidden from entering the assembly of God?
3. In what ways did Eliashib defile the sacred things of God?
4. Why do you think no one else stood up to rectify the wrongs that were being done?
5. What did Nehemiah do to restore the house of God?

6. In what ways can you compare the ministry and treatment of the Levites and musicians you know?

7. What steps did Nehemiah take to develop a sustainable plan to support the Levites?

ACTIVITY

Think of five ways you can help with the upkeep of your church and support the ministers. Commit to doing at least two of them.

NOTES

PRAYER # 9

The Holy Sabbath

Then I commanded the Levites to purify
themselves and go and guard the gates in order to
keep the Sabbath day holy.

Remember me for this also, my God, and show
mercy to me according to your great love
(Nehemiah 13:22).

In the absence of sound leadership chaos abounds. People do as they please. This is exactly what happened when Nehemiah was away from Jerusalem for a decade. After the wall was built and the people had experienced a revival, they committed to keeping God's commandments and to remain in covenant with Him. However, when Nehemiah returned, he found a spiritual dilemma. Apart from the high priest's betrayal of trust and evil doings and the injustice done to the Levites and musicians, Nehemiah watched as the people violated the covenant which they agreed to keep. The Jews were doing business with traders from all nations on the Sabbath. They were breaking the Ten Commandments specifically, "Remember the Sabbath day and keep it holy" (Exodus20:8). That was a serious indictment.

As Nehemiah observed their behavior, he was not only angry but grieved, knowing that Israel's failure to be obedient to God would incite His wrath and lead them again into the hands of their oppressors. How could they so easily forget that departure from God's ways led their forefathers into captivity? They had sinned against the same God who delivered them from Egypt into the Promised Land. In return, God asked for their faithful worship and obedience. History shows their repeated violations of God's laws. What Nehemiah was witnessing was no different.

Once again, the Israelites were conforming to the traditions and practices of the pagans. The Phoenicians and Tyrians did not observe the Sabbath; the Jews were in covenant with God to do so. Rather than remaining committed to their beliefs, they participated in the activities of the other nations on the Sabbath. Perhaps, it started on a small scale and then grew as they became more comfortable breaking the law.

The traders were, in fact, tempters of the Jews. They had no regard for the sacredness of the Sabbath day and encouraged the Israelites to break God's commandments by selling on that very day. They were deliberately oblivious to the potential destruction of the Jews. They cared only about their business and profit. If possible they would sell the skin of the teeth of the people. They were publicly disobeying God, to satisfy their pleasures. Unrestrained in their action all for financial advantage.

The scene in this chapter paints a vivid picture of what happens in our societies today. The church has adopted pagan customs, pagan holidays, and pagan beliefs. The Holy Sabbath is not observed as the day of rest which God appointed from creation. Could it be that the influence of the world is greater on the church than the church on the world? Ministers teach that the keeping of the Sabbath is no longer required by God. However, in Jeremiah 17:27, God gave a stern warning about violating the Sabbath:

> But if ye will not hearken unto me to hallow the
> Sabbath day, and not to bear a burden, even
> entering in at the gates of Jerusalem on the Sabbath

day; then will I kindle a fire in the gates thereof, and it shall devour the palaces of Jerusalem, and it shall not be quenched.

Nehemiah understood that the breaking of the Sabbath was not a trivial matter to be glossed over and excused. It was a violation of God's law. Yes, the people had found all types of excuses to justify their conformity to the pagan practice of not keeping the Sabbath. However, the truth remained, God Himself set aside the Sabbath day to be kept holy. He deemed it to be so important that it was included in the Ten Commandments the foundation of His covenant. Remember, we established that God gave the Ten Commandments to mankind to reveal His will and purpose for them and to show how we should relate to Him and our fellow humans. Therefore, given that the keeping of the Sabbath is one of the Ten Commandments, we can conclude that the keeping of the Sabbath is, indeed, the will and purpose for mankind and is applicable to the entire human race, not just the Jewish nation. The following excerpt explains further:

> When God reaffirmed the Sabbath for Israel, the Sabbath was more than a commandment; according to Exodus 31:13,17 (cp. Ezek 20:12), the Sabbath functioned as a sign of the covenant relationship by which he sanctified the Israelites. This function applied to Israel a principle which had been inherent in the Sabbath since Creation. On the seventh day of Creation, God sanctified the Sabbath (Gen 2:2-3), a unit of time. Why? In order to affect those who observe this special time. How would they be affected? They would emulate their holy Creator and acknowledge their on-going connection with him. Because they would belong to God, who is intrinsically holy, they would gain

holiness from him. In other words, the Sabbath would be a sign that God makes people holy, just as God explicitly said in Exodus 31:13 with particular reference to the Israelites. From the beginning, his desire has been for all people to enjoy a holy relationship with him.

The divine-human relationship signified by the Sabbath is one in which human beings are dependent upon God and his work. Thus, those who rest on the Sabbath acknowledge ". . . that I, the LORD, sanctify you . . ." (Exod 31:13) and "that in six days the LORD made heaven and earth" (vs. 17). The Sabbath is not simply the immovable "birthday of the world"; it recognizes the dependence of the world, and more particularly the human beings who have dominion over the world, on God who created the world.

Our dependence on God is not only based upon what he did for us thousands of years ago. According to the Bible, he continues to sustain his creatures. Speaking to King Belshazzar, Daniel referred to "the God in whose power is your very breath, and to whom belong all your ways" (Dan 5:23; cp. Ps 114:14-15; 145:15-16; Jb 12:10).

God will always be our Creator and Sustainer. Therefore, the basic meaning of the Sabbath, which encapsulates this divine-human relationship (cp. Cassuto 1967: 244), is timeless; it cannot become obsolete as long as human beings inhabit planet Earth

(Roy Gane is Associate Professor of Hebrew Bible and Ancient Near Eastern Languages in the Old Testament Department of the SDA Theological Seminary, Andrews University. Copyright 1997 *http://www.sdanet.org/atissue/covenants/ganecov .htm)*

Once again, Nehemiah had to take swift decisive action that would inevitably offend some people. Nehemiah locked the gates on the Friday night and never reopened them until the end of the Sabbath. This was to stop the trader who would set up their goods outside the gates from luring the Jews to come out and buy.

Nothing is written about the people or traders' response to this action. However, given human nature, we can imagine there were those who resisted change and the attempts of Nehemiah to make them comply with the laws of God. Nevertheless, Nehemiah was fearless. His priority was to honor God.

He threatened to arrest the traders and called heaven and earth as witnesses of what he would do if they did not leave. He was determined to stop them from disrespecting the Sabbath even if it meant compliance by force.

He also ordered the Levites to cleanse themselves and guard the gates. His efforts were successful. So in verse 22, much like in verse 14, he asked God to remember the things he did. He asked God to remember what he did. Restoring the keeping of the Sabbath highlights the importance of this day to God. Why would he ask God to remember him for doing something that had little or no meaning to Him?

In this prayer, Nehemiah adds a new dimension. He intimates there was pending judgment. He asks God to spare his life according to His mercy. He trusted in God's mercy to save him.

The request for salvation here was not based on Nehemiah's great works – there is no denying he had many. Instead, it was based on God's mercy.

The same applies to us. Though we like Nehemiah may accomplish great feats, we should never be presumptuous to think that any mercy God shows is because of our deeds. Salvation belongs to the Lord. It is not bought or sold by works or money. The price has already been paid. Hence, if you depend on good works, you will be sorely disappointed.

We have to beware of the tactics used by the world and even some in the church to lure us into being disobedient to God's Word and His commandments. We cannot allow the pagan world to make us idolaters, adulterers, coveters, Sabbath breakers or anything that violates God's purpose and will. Our attitudes and behaviors must be products of our beliefs. Like Nehemiah, let us hold fast and stand up for the truth despite the temptations, allurements, and popularity. In doing this, we will not be ashamed or afraid to ask God to remember the things we have done.

QUESTIONS

1. If you asked God to remember you according to what you have done with the Sabbath, what would be the outcome?
2. Why was Nehemiah so committed to defending the Sabbath and keeping it holy?
3. Why and when was the Sabbath established?
4. What decisive steps did Nehemiah take to stop the people from dishonoring God and His holy Sabbath?
5. What steps can you take to honor God and his holy Sabbath?

ACTIVITY

1. Which did is Gods Sabbath day today and give biblical support.

2. Would any six days of rest be acceptable to God in today world?

3. If the sabbath cannot save us by its keeping, what them is its relevance too today's Christian if any? (Exodus 20: 8-10)

NOTES

PRAYER # 10

Reforming the Priesthood

Remember them, O my God, because they have
defiled the priesthood, and the covenant of the
priesthood, and of the Levites (Nehemiah 13:29
KJV).

n the Old Testament, priests were chosen and
separated from the rest of the community by God to
carry out specific worship and sacrificial services in
the house of God. Joel 1:9 calls them "the Lord's
ministers." Priests were also mediators bridging the
gap between God and man. In the New Testament,
however, as part of the new covenant, Jesus became the only high
priest who mediates between God and man.

> For *there is* one God, and one mediator between
> God and men, the man Christ Jesus (1 Timothy
> 2:5).

The priests were also responsible for carrying out the day-to-day
operations in the temple. They offered the sacrifices and offerings
to God. They were the ones responsible for the sprinkling of the
blood, the burning of the offerings according to regulations, and
offering the sacrifice to God on behalf of the people. Their close
contact to the altar and most sacred places meant that the priests
were to be "holy to their God and not profane the name of the
Lord" (Leviticus 21:6). Leviticus 21:1-23 outlines several other
requirements of those who would enter the priesthood.

Given God's expectations, it is not surprising that Nehemiah was very distraught about what he saw. He returned to a place where the priests appeared to have lost their integrity, had no fear of God, and failed to set an example for the people. Their behaviour was similar to that of the people they led. It was one thing for the people to be contemptuous about God's laws, but an even more grievous matter that the priests themselves were doing the same. They defiled the priesthood and the covenant of the priesthood and of the Levites:

> The covenant of the priesthood. Not the covenant of the everlasting priesthood which God had granted to Phinehas (Num. 25:13), but the covenant God had concluded with the tribe of Levi and with Aaron and his descendants (Ex. 28:1). This covenant required the priests to be "holy unto their God" (Lev. 21:6, 8), who had chosen them to be ministers of His sanctuary and stewards of His grace (SDA Bible Commentary, *http://mediaset.sdasofia.org/*).

The end of Eli's sons and Eli himself is a warning to those who choose to be scoundrels in high office in the house of God. Hophni and Phinehas were priests at the tabernacle. Yet, they "knew not the Lord" (1 Samuel 2:12). In other words, they were wicked. They used the sacrifices of God for their own pleasure and had sex with the women at the entrance of the tabernacle. God warned them about their wickedness by sending two prophets with the same message. However, they refused to repent. God destroyed them and their father Eli on the same day.

Though the circumstances are different, the principle remains the same. The priests were consecrated to be holy representatives and outstanding men of God who kept the laws of God and taught the people to do so. However, like many in our times, they failed to live up to that holy calling.

Keeping the law was essential to Israel's existence. They could not succeed without God. Therefore, we see that their turning away to idolatry and breaking covenant often led to their captivity. This confirms that sin is a reproach to a nation. Clearly, because of the significant role the priest played, their sins and poor examples could not be taken lightly. They had the power to lead the entire nation astray. Hence, Nehemiah asked God to remember them knowing that their punishment had more far-reaching effects than simply disciplining them for their sins, but it was the opportunity for the nation to be renewed.

The Israelites started to intermarry again. The men took wives from foreign lands who served false gods. This was strictly forbidden by law and threatened to corrupt the priestly line (Leviticus 21:6-8, 14-15).

Exodus 34:15-16 details the covenant in which Israel agreed not to intermarry. The Israelite males marrying foreign women would be led astray to serve their foreign gods. King Solomon was a typical example of this.

> But king Solomon loved many strange women, together with the daughter of Pharaoh, women of the Moabites, Ammonites, Edomites, Zidonians, and Hittites:
>
> [2] Of the nations concerning which the LORD said unto the children of Israel, Ye shall not go in to them, neither shall they come in unto you: for surely they will turn away your heart after their gods: Solomon clave unto these in love (1 Kings 11:1-2).

King Solomon had a penchant for foreign women even though He knew God had forbidden such relationships. Inevitably, they turned his heart away from God. What made a wise king think that he could disobey God's will and not fall prey to the enemy? Was it the deceitfulness of sin and love of pleasures more alluring than a relationship with a loving God?

Solomon started his life with a genuine desire to please and worship God. His passion was expressed in his commitment to building the temple of God as He had ordained. As he dedicated the temple he said a remarkable prayer that revealed his desire to serve God faithfully (1 Kings 8:22-61). He ended it with these words, "And may your hearts be fully committed to the LORD our God, to live by his decrees and obey his commands, as at this time."

How did Solomon move from his devotion to obeying God's decrees to turning away from God? He embraced the things that God had forbidden. He opened his life to sin and eventually, it became easier to be disobedient. The Word of God had little or no effect. Solomon's life followed his heart ad his heart was with the gods of his foreign wives.

Solomon's spiritual demise is a lesson that we ought to diligently guard our hearts. Sin is deceitful and if we recklessly dabble in the forbidden, our hearts will also lead us far away from God. Solomon's love for his foreign wives negatively affected his love for God. The more he loved them the less he loved God.

As mentioned earlier, there is a direct correlation between our love for God and keeping His commandments. If you love God, you keep His commandments. It stands to reason, therefore, that loving sin and loving God cannot co-exist. We love one or the other.

Solomon started on the right path but sad to say, the man who vowed to keep God's laws and decrees was now pursuing and worshipping false gods in his old age.

> He followed Ashtoreth the goddess of the Sidonians, and Molech the detestable god of the Ammonites. So Solomon did evil in the eyes of the LORD; he did not follow the LORD completely, as David his father had done. On a hill east of Jerusalem, Solomon built a high place for Chemosh the detestable god of Moab, and for Molech the detestable god of the Ammonites. He did the same for all his foreign wives, who burned incense and offered sacrifices to their gods (1 Kings 11:5-8).

His apostasy was a serious offence. It was an affront to God. He abandoned and renounced the God of heaven, the God of his forefathers. God was very angry. The story of Solomon ended on a strikingly different note to when he began. Be careful not to let Solomon's story become yours where lust , greed and your love for sin turn your heart from God.

Like Solomon, the very priests who knew better broke God's law and married pagans in direct violation of the Law of Moses. They failed to set the right example for the people. They did exactly what God describes in Malachi 2:1-8:

> And now, O ye priests, this commandment is for you.

> If ye will not hear, and if ye will not lay it to heart, to give glory unto my name, saith the LORD of hosts, I will even send a curse upon you, and I will

curse your blessings: yea, I have cursed them already, because ye do not lay it to heart.

Behold, I will corrupt your seed, and spread dung upon your faces, even the dung of your solemn feasts; and one shall take you away with it.

And ye shall know that I have sent this commandment unto you, that my covenant might be with Levi, saith the LORD of hosts.

My covenant was with him of life and peace; and I gave them to him for the fear wherewith he feared me, and was afraid before my name.

The law of truth was in his mouth, and iniquity was not found in his lips: he walked with me in peace and equity, and did turn many away from iniquity.

For the priest's lips should keep knowledge, and they should seek the law at his mouth: for he is the messenger of the LORD of hosts.

But ye are departed out of the way; ye have caused many to stumble at the law; ye have corrupted the covenant of Levi, saith the LORD of hosts.

The priests had departed from God and caused many to stumble. Church leaders, ministers of the gospel, pastors and others who hold high office in churches should not ignore the severity of violating God's laws and making others fall. God does not take it lightly.

You can see why Nehemiah asked God not to remember. Nehemiah was asking God not to hold him responsible for what the priests did.

Today, the church battles with similar issues Nehemiah faced as a leader. There appears to be the absence of truth, honesty, integrity, and obedience to God's Word. Many people are being led astray by leaders who appear to be solely interested in increasing their fortunes. Compromise seems to be the order of the day. The Word of God is being neglected and replaced by the opinions and fancies of the leaders. Moral laxity is prevalent both in the pews and the pulpit. Yet, the same God who keeps covenant and shows mercy is reaching out to forgive if we are willing to repent. In the absence of repentance, there is judgment. God sent two prophets to warn Eli's sons. He sent also sent two warnings to King Solomon.

Nehemiah maintained his integrity and love for God. In verse 30, again he took steps to restore and correct the wrong. It was time for the priesthood to be restored to its rightful purpose and to perform services to the Lord. The priests themselves needed to be cleansed. They needed to function in their priestly offices as God had ordained to the benefit of the nation.

> So I purified the priests and the Levites of everything foreign, and assigned them duties, each to his own task (Nehemiah 13:30).

QUESTIONS
1. Why did Nehemiah ask God to remember the priests?
2. How was the priesthood defiled?
3. Why was the defilement of the priesthood such a bad thing for the nation of Israel?
4. How does sin impact our lives and our nation?
5. In verse 30, what steps did Nehemiah take to rectify the problem?

6. What have you learned from the prayers of Nehemiah that can transform your life?
7. How can following Nehemiah's example make you a better leader in general?

ACTIVITY

Commit to leading and living with integrity, humility, and to love God with all your heart, mind, and soul. Make prayer a priority in your life every day.

Conclusion

Nehemiah's story is filled with many valuable life lessons. His impeccable character, total confidence in God, passion for keeping God's commandments and ensuring the people and God's house were living and functioning according to purpose were defining. He was always a step ahead of his enemies, used excellent leadership skills to make things happen and created structures to ensure that the systems he put in place were sustained.

When other men turned the other way and ignored sin, Nehemiah stood up at the risk of being condemned, threatened and ostracized, *not only to call it out but to stamp it out.*

When the Levites were being wronged, when evil Tobiah had taken over the storerooms of the temple with the permission of Eliashib the high priest, Nehemiah stopped the corruption. He got rid of the traders who encouraged the Israelites to break the Sabbath and dealt with the priests who defiled the priesthood.

How did this man accomplish so much in the midst of threats, conspiracy, scandals, and deceit? Where did he find the strength to face each day knowing the troubles ahead?

As we studied Nehemiah we recognize a common thread in all that he did – prayer. Prayer strengthened him to complete the great assignment God gave him. Against the odds, he persevered and conquered. Likewise, when we recognize the power and importance of prayer to the God of heaven, we will find the strength and courage to win in the face of adversity.

God in His providence does not permit us to know the end from the beginning; but He gives us the light of His Word to guide us as we pass along, and bids us to keep our minds stayed upon Jesus. Wherever we are, whatever our employment, our hearts are to be uplifted to God in prayer. This is being instant in prayer. We need not wait until we can bow upon our knees, before we pray. On one occasion, when Nehemiah came in before the king, the king asked why he looked so sad, and what request he had to make. But Nehemiah dared not answer at once. Important interests were at stake. The fate of a nation hung upon the impression that should then be made upon the monarch's mind; and Nehemiah darted up a prayer to the God of heaven, before he dared to answer the king. The result was that he obtained all that he asked or even desired (Historical Sketches of the Foreign Missions of the Seventh-day Adventists, 144).

Appendix

In years past, I have spoken in favor of the plan of presenting our mission work and its progress before our friends and neighbors, and have referred to the example of Nehemiah. Now I urge our brothers and sisters to study anew the experience of this man of prayer and faith and sound judgment, who boldly asked his friend, King Artaxerxes, for help to advance the interests of God's cause (Manuscript 2, "Consecrated Efforts to Reach Unbelievers," June 5, 1914).

The experience of Nehemiah is repeated in the history of God's people in this time. Those who labor in the cause of truth will find that they cannot do this without exciting the anger of its enemies. Though they have been called of God to the work in which they are engaged, and their course is approved of Him, they cannot escape reproach and derision. They will be denounced as visionary, unreliable, scheming, hypocritical,—anything, in short, that will acquiesce to the purpose of their enemies. The most sacred things will be represented in a ridiculous light to amuse the ungodly. A very small amount of sarcasm and low wit, united with envy, jealousy, impiety, and hatred, is sufficient to excite the mirth of the profane scoffer. And these presumptuous jesters sharpen one another's ingenuity, and embolden each other in their blasphemous work. Contempt and derision are indeed painful to human nature; but they must be endured by all who are true to God. It is the policy of Satan thus to turn souls from doing the work which the Lord has laid upon them (The Southern Watchman, April 12, 1904).

Nehemiah and his companions did not shrink from hardships, or excuse themselves from trying service. Neither by night nor by day, not even during the brief time given to slumber, did they put off their clothing, or even lay aside their armor. "So neither I, nor my brethren, nor my servants, nor the men of the guard which followed me, none of us put off our clothes, saving that everyone put them off for washing" (The Southern Watchman, April 26, 1904).

The case of Nehemiah has been presented to me. He was not a man set apart for a priest or a prophet, but the Lord used him to do a special work. He was a leader of the people, but his fidelity to God did not rest upon his position (https://m.egwwritings.org).

To pray as Nehemiah prayed in his hour of need under circumstances when other forms of prayer may be impossible.
Toilers in the busy walks of life, crowded and almost overwhelmed with perplexity, can send up a petition to God for divine guidance. Travelers by sea and land, when threatened with some great danger, can thus commit themselves to Heaven's protection. In times of sudden difficulty or peril the heart may send up its cry for help to One who has pledged Himself to come to the aid of His faithful, believing ones whenever they call upon Him. In every circumstance, under every condition, the soul weighed down with grief and care, or fiercely assailed by temptation, may find assurance, support, and succor in the unfailing love and power of a covenant-keeping God (Prophets and Kings, 631, 632).

Over the countenance of any attendant of royalty. But in Nehemiah's seasons of retirement, concealed from human sight, many were the prayers, the confessions, the tears, heard and witnessed by God (Prayer, p. 149.2 Ellen Gould White)

Nehemiah's Prayers Were Braced With Firm Purpose—There is need of Nehemiah's in the church today,—not men who can pray and preach only, but men whose prayers and sermons are braced with firm and eager purpose.—(The Signs of the Times, December 6, 1883. Prayer, p. 150.3 Ellen Gould White https://m.egwwritings.org)

The success attending Nehemiah's efforts shows what prayer, faith, and wise, energetic action will accomplish. Living faith will prompt (SDA Bible Commentary, vol. 3 (EGW, p. 1137.1, Ellen Gould White https://m.egwwritings.org)

Four months Nehemiah waited to present his request to the king. Though his heart was heavy with grief, he endeavored to be cheerful in the royal presence. In those halls of luxury all must appear light-hearted and happy. But in Nehemiah's seasons of retirement, concealed from human sight, many were the prayers and tears heard and witnessed by God and angels (From Splendor to Shadow, p. 326.1, Ellen Gould White https://m.egwwritings.org).

About the Author

Paul A. Scavella has served as a pastor in the Seventh-day Adventist Church for 37 years. In 1975 he completed high school at Bahamas Academy in Nassau, Bahamas. Pastor Scavella continued studies for his college degree at Northern Caribbean University, formerly West Indies College in Mandeville Jamaica, where he obtained a Bachelor of Theology degree in 1979, with a minor in Biblical Languages. He later matriculated at Andrews University in Berrien Springs, Michigan where he obtained a Master's Degree in Divinity in 1985. In addition to Pastoral Ministry, he currently serves as the President of the South Bahamas Conference of Seventh-day Adventists.

Paul is married to Joan Marie. They have three adult children, Paul II, Paula-Jo, and Jo'Paul. Pastor Scavella is the President of Path to Life Vision Ministries, the co-founder of the Blossoming Place and a pioneer in the field of Biblical Coaching. These entities are avenues for blossoming individuals, churches, and organizations into their full potential for God's glory.

The following gives a glimpse into his mindset:

Motto: Serving with joy and gladness.

Mission Statement: Presenting Christ as the Path to Life for families, friends, and communities.

Vision Statement: To experience a walk with God and others on earth and in heaven.

Values:

Compassion	Honesty	Foundational -
Contact	Loyalty	Text: Psalm
Guiding	Love	16:11
Service	Excellence	
Respect	Justice for all	

AVAILABLE SOON!

Look out for Paul A. Scavella's next book **7S Imperatives for Natural Church Growth: Christ's Only True Methods,** which will soon be published. It is a remarkable book that presents practical, effective, and exciting strategies every church can use for church growth.

Made in the USA
Columbia, SC
14 November 2024

46286551R00054